# TIMES PAST
# GREATER
# MANCHESTER

LEFT TO RIGHT: STEAM WAGGON, 1957; ST ANN'S SQUARE, 1900; FASHION SHOW, KENDAL MILNE, 1956; WALKING OUT TO BAT, OLD TRAFFORD, 1938. BOTTOM: SALFORD ART GALLERY, PEEL PARK, 1880.

## ROBERT GIBB

MYRIAD
LONDON

# The City Centre

*Mancunium, a Roman fort, was sited at the crossroads of some of the most strategic routes in Britain. From this historic beginning the modern city of Manchester developed. The Industrial Revolution fuelled a tremendous growth in population and the city's fine Victorian architecture reflects its wealth and importance since that time*

ABOVE: **MARKET STREET, 1895.** Horse-drawn trams ferry passengers to and from the busy city centre. Destinations include Alexandra Park, Brooks Bar and Hyde Road. The pavements are heaving with shoppers and business people. Market Street was widened between 1822 and 1834 at a cost of £200,000.

ABOVE RIGHT: **MARKET STREET AND ITS JUNCTION WITH CROSS STREET, 1914.** Since the 13th century Market Street has been at the centre of the city's retail trade. The first horse-drawn omnibus service in Britain was started in 1824 between Pendleton and Market Street.

BELOW: **MARKET STREET, 1953.** Crowds of shoppers throng the city centre dodging traffic on the corner of Cross Street, looking up towards Piccadilly in the distance. The Arndale Centre now occupies the left-hand side of Market Street from Burton's the tailors to Debenhams in the distance.

RIGHT: **EXCHANGE STATION & CROMWELL'S STATUE,** *c* 1885. The imposing statue of Cromwell looks up Victoria Street. Erected in 1875, in 1968 it was moved to Wythenshawe Hall which, during the Civil War, Roundhead troops used as a billet. Exchange Station was demolished in the mid 1980s and replaced with a car park.

The Royal Infirmary was originally sited in Piccadilly Gardens before it moved to its present location in Oxford Road in 1908. BELOW: PICCADILLY, *c* 1890. The Royal Infirmary on the right-hand side casts a dark shadow over Piccadilly. On the corner of Mosley Street stands the statue of Robert Peel, erected in 1856, which looks towards Oldham Street. This was Manchester's first outdoor statue, financed by public subscription. Over £3,000 was collected in one week. LEFT: PICCADILLY, *c* 1910. The final stages of the demolition of the Royal Infirmary that was built on this site in 1775. Part of the building, which is still intact, is the accident room on Parker Street. The tower in the background is part of the Minshull Street law courts.

ABOVE: FIRE ALARM, 1959. Street fire alarms like this one sited at the junction of Spring Gardens and King Street were a novel way to summon the fire brigade when telephones were scarce. The alarms were taken out of service on April 1 1959.

ABOVE: PICCADILLY GARDENS, 1936. A view of the gardens from Portland Street looking towards Lewis's department store on the other side. The gardens were once a claypit until Lord Mosley donated the land for use as a public garden in the late 18th century.

RIGHT: **ALBERT SQUARE,** *c* **1922.** An aerial view of the Town Hall and surrounding buildings in Albert Square. The Gothic-style Town Hall was built between 1866-77 and designed by Alfred Waterhouse, the famous architect who also built the Natural History Museum in London. The interior of the building is richly decorated and includes murals by the pre-Raphaelite artist Ford Madox Brown.

BELOW: **ALBERT SQUARE,** *c* **1950.** Albert Square has a number of monumental statues. To the front of the Town Hall is the Albert Memorial, constructed in 1862-7 and designed by Thomas Worthington, the architect who was responsible for many of the area's outstanding public buildings.

Worthington's buildings include the nearby Memorial Hall facing Albert Square, the City Police Court and the Minshull Street Crown Court.

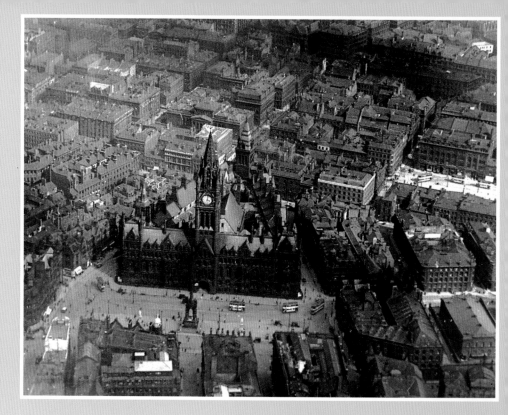

ABOVE: **FREE TRADE HALL, 1951.** The hall was built in 1856 and is one of the few buildings in the world to be named after a political or economic movement – one dear to the hearts of the city's 19th-century industrialists. It was almost entirely destroyed by bombing but re-opened as home to the City's Halle Orchestra from 1951-96.

LEFT: **THE ART GALLERY AND MOSLEY STREET, 1880.** A police officer stands at the junction of Princess Street and Mosley Street waiting to direct traffic. In the foreground is the Manchester Art Gallery. The building was designed by Charles Barry and opened in 1834; it has operated as the City Art Gallery since 1882.

Above: **The Royal Exchange, 1905.**
The Exchange was established to accommodate Manchester's cotton traders. The building shown here was completed in 1874 and is the third Exchange building on the site. In 1968 it ceased trading; the building today houses the Royal Exchange Theatre.

Right: **Manchester Central Library under construction, 1932.** The first library in Manchester was opened in 1852 at the Hall of Science (on the site of the current Air and Space Museum). The collection soon outgrew the premises and E Vincent Harris (1876-1971) won the competition to build the new library. It was opened in 1934 by King George V.

Below: **Manchester Cathedral, 1936.** The memorial service for the death of George V (1919-36). The King had been a regular visitor to Manchester particularly during the First World War and its aftermath.

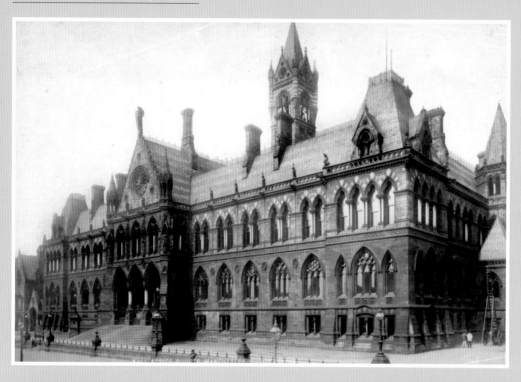

ABOVE: **ASSIZE COURTS**, *c* 1895. Begun in 1859 the Assize Courts were the first major work of Alfred Waterhouse (1830-1905) who also designed Manchester Town Hall. Located close to Strangeways Prison, the courts were constructed at a cost of over £13,000. The courts were badly damaged during the Blitz and were subsequently demolished.

BELOW: **THE MANCHESTER GUARDIAN BUILDING**, *c* 1905. The original Manchester Guardian and Manchester Evening News building stood opposite the Exchange building on Cross Street. The papers were printed in the basement and then rushed over to horse-drawn carts for distribution. In 1970 the building was demolished and the papers moved to new premises in Deansgate.

LEFT: **KING STREET,** *c* 1900. Most of the property on King Street consisted of business or professional accommodation. Houses had been steadily demolished during the preceding years to make way for prestigious office buildings and banks. In the distance the Manchester Reform Club displays traces of its Gothic architecture. Built between 1870-1 by Edward Salomons, it was one of the largest purpose-built club-houses outside London. A grand staircase runs the height of the building from the spacious entrance hall, and on the ground floor there are magnificent lavatories with marble washbasins.

ABOVE: **SPRING GARDENS,** *c* 1910. A busy scene on the cobbled Spring Gardens outside the Post Office. In the background is the new Midland Bank in its final stages of completion. This huge Art Deco-style building is clad in white stone and was designed by Sir Edwin Lutyens who also designed the Cenotaph in St Peter's Square.

ABOVE: **DEANSGATE, 1900.** Deansgate was the home of many quality shops, businesses and services. The Old Picture Shop displayed its paintings outside to catch the eye of passing customers.

LEFT: **AN AERIAL VIEW OF THE DEANSGATE DISTRICT** which clearly shows the City Exhibition Hall, St Matthew's and St John's churches, the Opera House, Sunlight House and, on the right, the LNER goods yard.

RIGHT: **CHETHAM'S SCHOOL, 1938.** Young boys in the dining hall of the famous school with its superb inglenook fireplace. This ancient manor house, which dates from 1421, is the most complete set of medieval buildings to survive in north-west England. It occupies the site of the manor house of Manchester which, together with the parish church (now the Cathedral), formed the core of the medieval town. It was saved from destruction by Humphrey Chetham whose bequest allowed for the renovation of the building and the establishment of a school to educate 40 poor children. In 1969 Chethams became a co-educational school for young musicians.

# Transport

*Manchester can lay claim to a clutch of British transport "firsts" – the first passenger railway line was the one from Manchester to Liverpool, served by the first passenger railway station at Liverpool Road. Barton Airport was the UK's first municipal airport and the Manchester Ship Canal was the first canal to link ocean-going ships to an inland British city*

Above: **Horse-drawn omnibus, 1880.** Operating the route from Cheadle to Manchester via Didsbury, this privately-owned carriage could carry up to 42 passengers bound for the city centre. Twelve passengers had to brave the elements by sitting on the upper deck.

Left: **Deansgate, 1901.** A crowd of trackmen gather round the newly-laid St Mary's Gate junction on Deansgate – a vital part of the city's first electric-powered tramway from Albert Square to Cheetham Hill.

Below left: **Albert Square, 1901.** The official opening of the electric tramway on June 6 1901 was attended by thousands of spectators and officials, the crowds controlled by numerous police officers. Over 500 new trams were used between 1901 and 1903. The Queen's Road depot accommodated over half the vehicles and Hyde Road depot was built to house the balance.

Right: **Piccadilly bus station, 1935.** Passengers wait patiently in the rain for services at the Piccadilly Gardens bus station.

Far right: **Trafford Road Bridge, 1894.** The Swing Bridge was one of seven bridges built to span the Manchester Ship Canal. Built in 1892 by Butler and Co of Leeds, it was the smallest bridge on the canal but, at 1,800 tons, the heaviest. Just beyond the bridge is Pomona Dock.

RIGHT: **MANCHESTER AIRPORT, 1930.** Airport dignitaries await the arrival of Lady Bailey, one of the pioneering figures in women's aviation, for the King's Cup air race around England. Established by King George V as an incentive for the development of British light aircraft and engine design, the event was watched by more than 30,000 people. Lady Bailey (1890-1960) was one of the pioneering figures in women's aviation. She was the first woman to fly across the Irish Sea, and in 1928 made an epic solo flight from Croydon to Cape Town and back.

ABOVE: **CHAT MOSS AERODROME, 1931.** Film actress Frances Day poses with a de Havilland DH60X Moth with the emblem of Manchester Airport painted on its fuselage.

BELOW: **MANCHESTER AIRPORT, 1932.** The City Council wanted to be the first in Britain to have a licensed airfield and Barton was chosen to replace an earlier airfield at Alexandra Park when the landowner refused to sell the site. Barton opened in 1930 and included a control tower and large hangar. With only a grass runway it soon became unsuitable for larger aircraft and an area south of Manchester was earmarked for development. Named Ringway, it took three years to construct and opened in June 1938.

INSET: **COLLECTING THE LICENCE FOR BARTON AIRPORT, 1929.** On April 22 two aircraft carried a civic delegation including the Lord Mayor, Col George Westcott, to Croydon to collect a temporary licence for the new airport at Barton.

LEFT: **MANCHESTER AIRPORT, c 1950.** In the golden age of air travel there were very few passengers. Compared with today, when more than 150,000 passengers a year pass through the departure lounge, this photograph of the main reception area at Ringway shows how few people travelled by air at this time.

# INDUSTRY AND MANUFACTURING

*Manchester has long been at the heart of Britain's manufacturing industry with "works" for every kind of product — from locomotives at the famous Gorton Tank in Openshaw, to motor vehicles, aircraft and newspaper production. But it was the cotton boom of the nineteenth century that fuelled the city's expansion and brought the great wealth which is evident today in the city's fine buildings — from Victorian textile mills to modernist gems such as the Express building in Ancoats*

RIGHT: **CROSSLEY WORKS, OPENSHAW, 1934.** This important company was founded by Francis and William Crossley in 1867 and employed many skilled craftsmen. Here motor bus bodies are being painted in the workshop before they are fitted to the chassis. INSET: **CROSSLEY ELECTRIC BATTERY VEHICLE, 1935.** Development work on these electric-powered vehicles stopped before the Second World War when the firm shifted production to the manufacture of military vehicles.

LEFT: **OLD TRAFFORD,** *c* 1920. H&J Quick, an authorised Ford dealer, refuels a car on the forecourt.
BELOW: **HULME, 1907.** The first car built by Rolls Royce in 1904, parked in Cooke Street. This car sold for £395 when it was built; today it is valued at approximately £250,000. The famous radiator badge, known as "The Spirit of Ecstasy", was based on Eleanor Thornton, the secretary and mistress of Lord Montague of Beaulieu, a Rolls Royce customer.

ABOVE: **MANCHESTER SHIP CANAL, 1929.** Locomotives from the Beyer Peacock railway works (known locally as Gorton Tank) waiting to be loaded onto ships for delivery around the world and, right, being craned into position. The works at Gorton Foundry on Railway Street began production in 1854 and manufactured more than 8,000 locomotives. The works closed in 1966; today the buildings are used as a depot for Manchester Corporation.

Left: **THE OFICES OF THE DAILY HERALD, OXFORD STREET,** *c* **1930.** Sub-editors prepare copy before the paper goes to press. Launched in 1911, the *Daily Herald* moved to its Oxford Street premises in 1930. The paper was set up in the aftermath of a printworkers strike and became the voice of the labour movement. It was the only newspaper to fully support the suffragettes.

Below left: **ANCOATS,** *c* **1939.** Reels of paper arrive on wagons at the *Daily Express* building in Ancoats. This impressive glass structure was designed by Sir Owen Williams and built in 1939. It is one of the first examples of the Modernist style in Manchester. The triple height rooms on the ground floor were built to accommodate the printing presses.

Below right: **THE CROSS STREET OFFICES OF THE MANCHESTER GUARDIAN AND EVENING NEWS, 1957.** The papers were based at Cross Street from 1886 until their move, in 1970, to Deansgate. The Cross Street building was demolished in 1972.

Below: **AERIAL VIEW OF MOSTON, 1935.** The electronics giant Ferranti moved to the north-west from London, tempted by lower land costs and wages. Pioneering work on the development of computers was done at Moston in collaboration with the University of Manchester. The Ferranti archive was based at Moston until 1990.

# COTTON

*For more than a century the Lancashire cotton industry was the most important in the world and many of the towns to the north of Manchester expanded rapidly as a result of the rising demand for cotton goods. Work in the mills bred an independence of spirit which survives to this day*

ABOVE: **CLOVER MILL, ROCHDALE, 1952.** The great fire at the mill on June 5 1952 caused over £1m of damage. More than 250 firemen battled for nine hours to extinguish the blaze, thought to have started when a blow-lamp exploded in the basement.

ABOVE: **SAMUEL CROMPTON'S BIRTHPLACE, FIRWOOD FOLD, BOLTON 1940.** Samuel Crompton (1753-1827) invented the spinning mule in 1799 – a machine which revolutionised the Lancashire cotton industry by enabling cloth to be produced much more quickly than previously.

RIGHT: **AN AERIAL VIEW OF THE SHIRLEY INSTITUTE, DIDSBURY, 1936.** The institute was set up by the British Cotton Research Association and given the name Shirley after the daughter of a Stockport MP, William Greenwood. The first purpose-built laboratories at the institute were opened in 1922 by the Duke of York. The Victorian house north of the laboratories played a key role in the history of Manchester: named The Towers it was originally owned by Edward John Taylor, the proprietor of the *Manchester Guardian*. In 1874 it was bought by the engineer Daniel Adamson and in 1882 a meeting was held in the house at which the decision to build the Manchester Ship Canal was taken.

## COTTON PRODUCTION, MANCHESTER, BOLTON AND ROCHDALE, c 1934.

In the 1830s approximately 85 per cent of all cotton manufactured worldwide was produced in Lancashire. Despite periodic slumps, by the 1930s the industry was still an important employer. Fabric production involved turning raw cotton, usually imported from the USA via Liverpool, into finished cloth. Many of the hot and dirty activities were performed by women who were overseen by male machine operators. The aristocrats of the cotton industry were the "mule-spinners" – skilled male workers who earned a "family" wage and whose wives did not have to go out to work. For those women who worked alongside men, earning a wage meant that they became known for their independence and self-reliance, and many Lancashire women campaigned for radical causes – from votes for women to equal pay.

# LEISURE AND PLEASURE

*Sport and leisure have always played a major role in Manchester life, the home of two famous top-class football teams as well as Lancashire Cricket Club. For more than one hundred years the city also possessed Belle Vue – the greatest outdoor attraction in Britain and the forerunner of today's theme parks*

ABOVE: **BELLE VUE, 1946.** In the aftermath of the Second World War, Belle Vue had record visitor numbers – there was a new sense of freedom now that the war was over. In the crowd (above) a number of servicemen can be seen enjoying a day out while home on leave.
RIGHT: **BELLE VUE, 1903.** Buffalo Bill and his Wild West Circus were regular visitors to Belle Vue. Their show included portrayals of a buffalo hunt, an Indian attack and Custer's last stand.

ABOVE: **CAESAR'S PALACE** saw many uses throughout its life, first as a restaurant, then as a hotel and lastly as a public house. The front elevation of the building collapsed in 1980 and the rest of the building was then demolished.
BELOW: **AERIAL PHOTOGRAPH OF THE GIANT BELLE VUE SITE, 1922.** In the foreground are the caterpillar and "bobs" and in the distance the boating lake, at the centre of which was the famous Jennison clock tower. It was named after John Jennison who started the park in 1836 and was demolished in 1949. A windmill was erected in its place. In 1963 the lake was drained and filled in.

ABOVE: **BELLE VUE, 1900.** Among the many attractions of the amusement park was the "figure of eight" with its toboggan rides which dominated the skyline. But as maintenance costs rose and newer rides became more popular, so the "bobs" were demolished.
RIGHT: **BELLE VUE KEEPER, 1920.** The monkey terrace was added to the side of the elephant house in the late 1890s. The chimps' tea party was always a firm favourite with children.

LEFT: **OLD TRAFFORD, 1959.** Manchester United moved from their old ground at Bank Street, Clayton to a brand new stadium at Old Trafford. For its day, Old Trafford was a state of the art facility with terracing on three sides and a covered main stand with seating. The ground was badly bomb-damaged during the Second World War and United played their home games at Maine Road from 1946-49.

RIGHT: **FA CUP FINAL, WEMBLEY, 1934.** Sam Cowan, Manchester City captain, accepts the trophy after the team's victory over Portsmouth in 1934. Sam was appointed player-manager at Mossley in 1937. He died in 1964 aged 62 after collapsing while refereeing a charity cricket match in aid of wicket-keeper Jim Parks.

BELOW: **OLD TRAFFORD, 1930.** Manchester United FC was founded in 1892 and joined the league that year. Previously called Newton Heath from 1893-1902 the team shown here finished twenty-second in League Division 1 with 22 points.

RIGHT: **MAINE ROAD, 1950.** Bert Trautmann, City's famous German goalkeeper, is swamped by autograph-hunters outside the Maine Road ground. Trautmann spent part of the war at a POW camp in Ashton and was brought to the club in 1949 by manager John Thomson – a highly controversial move which sparked a demonstration of 40,000 people on the city streets. Trautmann eventually won the hearts and minds of the fans and was awarded the OBE in 2004.

RIGHT: **OLD TRAFFORD CRICKET GROUND, 1957.** The Warwick Road ground hosted a three-day match that summer between Lancashire and the West Indies. The Windies won by nine wickets.

LEFT: **MARKET STREET,** *c* 1950. The Church of England Whit Sunday walk parades down Market Street. Whit Walks took place at Whitsuntide – the seventh Sunday after Easter – when children carrying posies and banners paraded from their churches to the city centre. It was customary to wear a new outfit for the occasion. Thousands of people lined the streets to watch, bringing the city centre to a standstill.

# THE CITY AT WAR

*Manchester played a key role in both world wars and sent large numbers of troops and armaments to the front. As a centre of heavy industry the city suffered badly from bombing during the Second World War. In true tradition, Manchester's people rallied round to protect the vulnerable and help to defeat the enemy*

RIGHT: **ALBERT SQUARE, 1915.** Lord Kitchener visits Manchester. Kitchener had completely reorganised the army into 69 divisions by April 1915, 30 of whch were made up of volunteers, many from Manchester and Liverpool.

ABOVE: **USA TANK BOYS, SALFORD DOCKS, 1914.** Although American forces did not enter the First World War until April 1917, the USA regularly sent boats with equipment and specialist help to the Allies throughout the early years of the war.

RIGHT: **EVACUATION, 1939.** During September 1939, 72,000 children and 32,000 adults were voluntarily evacuated from the city. Some went as far afield as the Lake District but many only moved to the edge of the city to avoid the worst of the bombing.

ABOVE: **COLLYHURST, 1940.** In true Dad's Army fashion, a proud Home Guard battalion marches through Collyhurst. These volunteers had been promised uniforms and arms but, as can be seen here, their uniform consisted of little more than a roughly-made armband and their weapons amounted to a collection of pitchforks, broomsticks and makeshift rifles.

LEFT AND ABOVE: **CHURCHILL VISIT, DECEMBER 1940.** The air raids on the nights of December 22-23 were particularly bad, killing over 700 people and badly damaging Manchester Cathedral, Old Trafford football ground and the Royal Exchange. The Free Trade Hall (left) was ruined. Winston Churchill (above) visited the scene of devastation at the Free Trade Hall and St Peter's Street after the December raids.

Between July 1940 and June 1941 the Manchester area suffered a number of devastating air raids which included one on Salford (below).

RIGHT: **WARTIME PICCADILLY, 1940.** During the war the gardens were transformed into giant bomb shelters. Despite civil defences such as these there was heavy loss of life in the Manchester Blitz. News of civilian casualties and damage to areas such as Trafford Park was kept out of the news by order of the Government so as not to spread despondency and alarm among the city's population.

RIGHT: **GAS GUZZLER, 1939.** This *Manchester Evening News* photograph from early on in the war shows one of the first cars to be converted to run on gas.

LEFT: **MANCHESTER CORPORATION BUS, 1942.** Three years into the war petrol rationing was beginning to bite. As an experiment some buses were converted to run on gas. However these buses had a poor reputation and often broke down.

*Originally a collection of separate towns and villages, the many districts around the city gradually merged into one urban area. Each district retained its own distinctive character: the areas to the north of the centre reflect much of the city's industrial past, while the leafy southern side, which was originally home to the wealthy cotton barons and industrialists, soon became the fashionable place to live for Manchester's middle-class professionals*

RIGHT AND BELOW LEFT: **TWO VIEWS OF CRUMPSALL.** The first, an aerial view from 1925 is of Crumpsall, Manchester and Prestwich hospital; the British Dyestuffs Corporation and Crumpsall Vale are in the background. The hospital was built between 1866-70 and was designed by the architect Thomas Worthington(1826-1909). Originally the Prestwich Union workhouse, the buildings are now part of the North Manchester General Hospital. The second, a postcard from 1924, is of the Church of St Matthew with St Mary, Cleveland Road.

ST. MATTHEW'S CHURCH, CRUMPSALL.

CRAB LANE

LEFT: **MOSTON BOTTOMS, 1934.** The Irk Valley region was a mining community and contained many small cottages. This was the original home of the Moston Brook animal sanctuary which flourished in the 1950s.

**TWO VIEWS OF BLACKLEY.** Crab Lane, above, in 1908 and Booth Hall Children's Hospital, left, c 1959. The Booth Lane Infirmary was built in 1907 using rubble from the house of local philanthropist Humphrey Booth. In 1914 the hospital developed a children's unit which rapidly became one of the leading children's hospitals in the country.

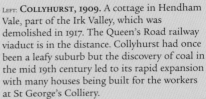

LEFT: **COLLYHURST, 1909.** A cottage in Hendham Vale, part of the Irk Valley, which was demolished in 1917. The Queen's Road railway viaduct is in the distance. Collyhurst had once been a leafy suburb but the discovery of coal in the mid 19th century led to its rapid expansion with many houses being built for the workers at St George's Colliery.

BELOW: **HARPURHEY, 1934.** Postmen pass the time of day at the junction of Rochdale Road and Queens Road.

LEFT: **ANCOATS, 1958.** This photograph was taken in the New Cross area of the town near the junction of Oldham Road. St Paul with St Michael and St Thomas Church and the Midland Bank can be seen.

RIGHT: **BESWICK, 1934.** Until the end of the Second World War housing in Beswick and neighbouring Ancoats largely consisted of streets of Victorian and Edwardian terraces like the one shown in the photograph. After the war much of this housing was demolished.

RIGHT: **ARDWICK, 1906.** Nicholls Hospital on Hyde Road was built between 1879-1880 for the education of poor boys. Its architect was Thomas Worthington — the runner-up in the competition to build Manchester Town Hall. It was financed from a bequest by Benjamin Nicholls, the son of a local mill-owning family, who died at the age of 36. During the Second World War it was used as a barracks for troops and the pupils were transferred to Chethams School. In 2002 the building was magnificently restored and is now the Manchester College for Arts and Technology.

BELOW: **ARDWICK, 1934.** The busy Stockport Road close to the junction with Devonshire Street.

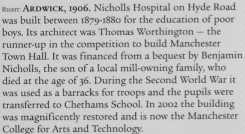

ABOVE: **CLAYTON, 1928.** A tram glides along the cobbled surface of Ashton New Road as people cross near the handsome Conservative Club. The Industrial Revolution propelled Clayton from a small village into a hive of industry. Its position close to the Ashton Canal meant that it was an important link in the transport network.

RIGHT: **BESWICK, 1963.** This view of children on the corner of Bowness Street could have come straight from *Coronation Street*.

ABOVE: **SUNNYBROW PARK, GORTON** *c* 1906. Adults and children enjoy the pleasures of the park. In the distance is Brookfield Unitarian Church built in 1870 and endowed by Richard Peacock, an engineer who became Gorton's first MP.

RIGHT: a rush cart outside the **PLOUGH HOTEL, GORTON,** *c* 1910. In the week before the annual rush-bearing ceremony in the local churches, a cart was taken round each of the local hotels and pubs in turn. On the day itself, fresh rushes were laid in each church and the old rushes burnt along with the cart.

LEFT: **STOCKPORT ROAD, LONGSIGHT, 1958.** Longsight developed alongside the ancient road between Buxton and Manchester (the A6). At the junction of Slade Lane and the Stockport Road was a tollbooth around which other buildings soon gathered. By 1960, the Longsight Free Christian Church (above) was being used by the BBC as a depot. Here an outside broadcast van sets off in search of a story.

LEFT: **LEAF STREET BATHS, HULME, 1920.** Built in 1860 the architect was Thomas Worthington, who also designed Manchester's Albert Memorial and the Nicholls Hospital. Along with Turkish baths and more conventional "single" baths, Leaf Street also boasted a laundry and spin-dryers — facilities vital for much of the local community who were without adequate baths and lavatories at home.

LEFT: **GROCER'S SHOP, HULME, 1939.** In the days before superstores, corner shops like the one seen here flourished. They provided everything from cooked meat and cheese to yeast and snuff.

ABOVE: **TRAFFORD PARK, c 1910.** By the early years of the 20th century the Ship Canal was helping to bring new prosperity to Manchester. Within 10 years of its opening more than 40 companies had moved to the newly established Trafford Park industrial estate, establishing this as the world's first industrial park. By 1945 the park employed over 75,000 workers. The triumphal arch (above) was erected for a trade exhibition.

LEFT: **NEW SCHOOL, MOSS SIDE, 1893.** Crowds gather round the site of the Princess Road Board School to watch the ceremony of the laying of the foundation stone. The size of the gathering shows the importance of the occasion for the local community.

LEFT: **AERIAL VIEW, RUSHOLME, 1925.** From the 1830s onwards Rusholme changed from being a quiet agricultural village to a busy Manchester suburb. Once the railway arrived in the mid-1850s, followed by the horse trams in 1880, house-building increased dramatically. The photograph above was taken in 1922 on Wilmslow Road looking towards Dickenson Road with Platt Fields in the distance. The Birch Vale Hotel on the left was a popular retreat.

RIGHT: **CHORLTON GREEN, 1928.** The Horse and Jockey pub overlooking the picturesque green; it acquired its half-timbered facade around 1910.

LEFT: **ZETLAND ROAD, CHORLTON, 1959.** The corner of Zetland Road, Sandy Lane and Barlow Moor. The handsome Zetland Terrace built in 1883 dominates the view.

ABOVE: **LEVENSHULME, 1907.** The suburb of Levenshulme is situated on the Manchester to Stockport Road. In the centre of the picture is the Levenshulme Town Hall. The council offices were moved in 1950 when the town was incorporated into the City of Manchester. The building is now the Levenshulme Antiques Village.

RIGHT: **WITHINGTON,** *c* **1910.** A view towards Withington village from the junction of Parsonage Road. The library is in the distance.

BELOW: **WITHINGTON,** *c* **1950.** The same view of the village 40 years later, this time looking down the road from the library, shows an increase in private cars and an absence of tramlines.

RIGHT: **BURNAGE,** *c* **1910.** Described by George Bernard Shaw as the prettiest village in Manchester, Burnage Garden Village — a garden suburb — was built with many new semi-detached houses and recreational facilities including a village hall, allotments, tennis courts and a children's playground. The garden village was completed in 1912 and soon became a fashionable suburb for professional people and their families.

*A corner of Old Didsbury.*

LEFT: **DIDSBURY, c 1935.** The Didsbury Hotel and Ye Olde Cock Inn, built in 1910, stand either side of the entrance to Fletcher Moss House and Gardens. The gateway was bought for £10 when the Spread Eagle Hotel was demolished.

BELOW LEFT: **GALLEON POOL, DIDSBURY, 1953.** Adults and children enjoy the outdoor Galleon Pool in Didsbury, not far from Parrs Wood junction. The area has now been developed as an hotel and leisure club.

BELOW: **CINEMA, NORTHENDEN, 1959.** The ABC or Forum cinema opened in 1934 and contained a Wurlitzer organ. In addition to all the film favourites of the day it also put on many stage shows.

RIGHT: **WYTHENSHAWE HALL, c 1920.** This Tudor half-timbered house was the home of the Tatton family for over 400 years. Built around 1540, the family sold most of the surrounding land for housing development to Manchester City Council in 1926. The Hall is still open for visitors today.

BELOW: **FISHMONGERS, NORTHENDEN, 1959.** On the corner of Brett Street, formerly Brown Street on Palantine Road, stands MacFisheries, the famous seafood shop. Many older residents remember the tiled floors and marble counters.

BELOW RIGHT: **SHADY LANE, BAGULEY, 1945.** Until the 1920s, Wythenshawe was a rural area dotted with small hamlets. Today one of the few reminders of the past is Baguley Hall which stands in the middle of a heavily built-up housing estate.

# SURROUNDING TOWNS

*Greater Manchester is made up of two cities, Manchester and Salford, and eight metropolitan boroughs — Trafford, Tameside, Bolton, Bury, Oldham, Rochdale, Stockport and Wigan. Although they are close geographically, each town is fiercely independent and retains its own distinct character and traditions*

ABOVE: **WIGAN, 1893.** A meal is provided for all the children at Ince Colliery near Wigan. Hundreds of pies are stacked on trestle tables waiting to be consumed by hordes of hungry youngsters.

RIGHT: **HAIGH HALL, WIGAN, 1950.** Once the property of the Lindsay family who owned a number of coalmines and iron foundries, Haigh Hall was built between 1827 and 1840. The hall is set in 250 acres of wood and parkland, much of it laid out in 1860 by local people temporarily unemployed during the Cotton Famine caused by the American Civil War.

ABOVE: **CINEMA OPENING VOTE, WIGAN, 1947.** Local people line up to vote on whether Manchester cinemas should be allowed to open on Sunday. The turnout for the vote was low — around 5 per cent in some areas.
BELOW: **COAL-PICKING, WIGAN,** *c* 1890S. Women grading coal at a colliery near Wigan.

ABOVE: **BURY, 1932.** Coke ovens were used for roasting coal. This drove off all the chemical constituents and reduced it to almost pure carbon or coke.

RIGHT: **SALFORD DOCK NUMBER 7,** *c* 1898. In 1894 the Manchester Ship Canal was opened, allowing boats to reach Pomona Docks just a mile from Manchester city centre. Larger docks were soon built half a mile west at Salford. A century later the docks were closed and the area redeveloped for housing and leisure. It is now known as Salford Quays.

RIGHT: **BOLTON TECHNICAL COLLEGE, 1955.** The first technical college in the town, the Bolton Mechanics Institute, opened in 1824 and the Crompton Literary and Scientific Institute was built in 1868. In 1946 Bolton Technical College was built. In 1982 the town's colleges formed the Bolton Institute of Higher Education, formally designated a university in 2005.

BELOW: **PEEL BUILDING, SALFORD, 1910.** In 1896 Salford Working Men's College and the Pendleton Mechanics joined forces to create the Salford Technical Institute. It was housed in the magnificent Peel Building in Peel Park. At the first session 1,240 students registered. The painter LS Lowry learned his artistic trade there and spent 22 years, mostly in evening classes, at the college. A few years later the college was renamed the Royal Technical Institute and in 1967 the Institute became part of the University of Salford.

LEFT: **FLAT IRON MARKET, SALFORD, 1894.** The Flat Iron Market, around Sacred Trinity Church, got its name from the triangular piece of land on which it was held. In 1939 the market closed and moved to Cross Lane in the centre of the town.

ABOVE: **SALFORD DISPENSARY, 1892.** In 1827 the first dispensary (a cross between a doctor's surgery and a hospital) was opened in the centre of the town. The population of the area was rising so quickly that the dispensary was moved in 1831 to larger premises and re-named the Salford and Pendleton Royal Dispensary. The dispensary became part of the Salford Royal Hospital in 1896.

RIGHT: **WAR MEMORIAL, BURY, 1920.** The Lancashire Fusiliers (now the Fusiliers) based at their headquarters in Bolton Road have had close connections with Bury since their formation more than 300 years ago. The Bury War Memorial (the "shouting fusilier") commemorates those members of the regiment who died during the Boer War of Higher Education, formally designated a university in 2005.

BELOW: **FIRE FIGHTING, BURY, 1960.** A large crowd of local residents gather to watch firefighters tackle a huge blaze at the Apex bedding factory in Bury.

ABOVE: **TOWN HALL, ROCHDALE, 1955.** The Gothic-style town hall was built in 1871 at a total cost of £160,000. The main tower was burnt down in 1883 and Alfred Waterhouse, the architect of Manchester Town Hall, was employed to replace it. The new tower was completed in 1890.

RIGHT: **FACTORY VISIT, BURY, 1931.** A trade visit of the staff of the children's shoe department from Lewis's in Manchester to Shepherd's shoe and slipper factory. The staff enjoyed a buffet lunch later at the Derby Hotel.

LEFT: **STATUE OF JOHN BRIGHT, ROCHDALE, 1909.** John Bright (1811-1889) was born in Rochdale, the son of a mill-owner. He joined Richard Cobden in the successful fight to repeal the Corn Laws and reduce tax on basic essentials imported to the country. John Bright was a Member of Parliament from 1843 until his death.

RIGHT: **ROCHDALE CANAL, 1954.** The Rochdale Canal company's boat *Roach,* seen here moored in the Rochdale basin.

LEFT: **CENTRAL ROCHDALE, 1935.** An aerial view of Rochdale Town Hall and the surrounding town centre. Rochdale can trace its history back to the Domesday Book of 1086. The medieval church of St Chad's on Sparrow Hill overlooks the town and dates back more than 1,000 years. Certain parts of the church are of Saxon origin. Rochdale is also home to the Co-operative Movement. The Rochdale Equitable Pioneers Society opened their first store in Toad Lane in 1844 — now the site of the Rochdale Pioneers Museum.

BELOW: **BUCKLEY HALL, ROCHDALE, 1900.** The Buckley Hall Brothers of Charity Orphanage and Industrial School was built in 1888 and operated until 1947. The area is now the site of HMP Buckley Hall. Built in 1970, it has been a women's prison since 2002.

BOTTOM: **CLOGGER, ROCHDALE, 1960.** A clogger at work in his dimly lit workshop. Cloggers would repair and manufacture the clogs which were worn by many of the local factory and farmworkers. They were a robust yet cheap form of footwear and helped protect the wearer's feet from heavy machinery.

ABOVE: **ROCHDALE HORNETS, 1950.** Formed in 1871, Rochdale Hornets were founder members of the Rugby League. The club were at their strongest in the first two decades of the 20th century and won the Challenge Cup in the 1921-22 season. For most of their history until 1988 the Hornets played at the famous Athletics Ground.

BELOW: **ROCHDALE HORNETS GRANDSTAND CRASH, 1939.** Tragedy struck at the Athletics Ground on April 1 when the main stand collapsed. Two spectators were killed and 15 others injured. The ground was packed when the roof of the stand gave way under the weight of spectators climbing onto it to get a better view.

RIGHT: **OLDHAM MUMPS STATION,** *c* 1920. The name of the railway station and the surrounding area probably derived from the archaic word "mumper" which was slang for a beggar.

BELOW: **OLDHAM ALMSHOUSE,** *c* 1890. The inhabitants of Oldham almshouse don their best clothes for a group photograph. Almshouses were built to house older people who were beyond working age and did not have the means to support themselves. They were often founded by philanthropic organisations and run by religious groups.

LEFT: **UNION STREET, OLDHAM, 1911.** Along with Triumph and Rover, Bradbury and Co of Oldham were one of the star names of the early motorcycle industry. Their agent in Oldham, Percy Platt, ran a shop selling motorcycles at 129 Union Street. Percy was himself a keen motorbike racer and won the Bradbury Cup, named after the manufacturer, on a 6hp sports model.

RIGHT: **PICTORIAL ACCIDENT, OLDHAM, 1950.** This photograph appeared in the local paper and showed how a young boy climbed the fire escape at the side of the cinema on Huddersfield Road, walked along the parapet and then fell through the glass canopy over the main entrance.

RIGHT: **TRAIN DERAILMENT, OLDHAM, 1907.** In 1759 Francis Egerton, the third Duke of Bridgewater, built the first commercial canal to bring coal from his pit at Worsley into Manchester. Worsley coal was used to fire the steam-driven machinery in the local mills and by the mid 19th century Oldham became one of the world's leading cotton-spinning towns. After the canals came the railways; here railway accident investigators examine the scene of a derailment to determine the cause and decide on a repair strategy at Cowhill near Chadderton. The engine and most of the carriages were badly damaged.

LEFT: **DAISY NOOK, ASHTON-UNDER-LYNE, 1941.** The small hamlet of Waterhouses is in Daisy Nook, a local beauty spot bordering the river Medlock between Ashton and Oldham. The hamlet was popularised in the short story *A Day Out* written by the early Victorian poet Ben Brierley.

BELOW LEFT: **STALEY HALL, STALYBRIDGE, 1898.** Staley Hall was the Tudor residence of the Staveleigh family and was built in the 16th century from locally-quarried stone.

BELOW: **ASHTON OLD HALL, ASHTON-UNDER-LYNE, c 1880.** Ashton Old Hall stood between the present by-pass and the railway. It was the home of the Assheton family and was built on ground once occupied by a fort commissioned for the King of Northumberland. The hall was compulsorily purchased in 1893 by the local railway company and demolished.

BELOW: **STALYBRIDGE, c 1966.** In 1845 the Sheffield, Aston and Manchester railway opened a new branch line from Guide Bridge in Ashton to Stalybridge. It was the first railway station in the area; here we see a steam engine and train passing through the station in full steam.

RIGHT: **ASHTON-UNDER-LYNE, 1959.** In the past, cotton was Ashton's most important industry. Today, most of the old mills have now been converted or demolished.

ABOVE: **TOLL BOOTH, STOCKPORT, 1929.** The Heaton Chapel toll-house on Wellington Road North was originally built to collect charges for vehicles using the local roads. The toll-house became a branch of the District Bank in the 1930s.

ABOVE: **UNDERBANK HALL, STOCKPORT, 1929.** Built in the latter part of the 15th century, Underbank Hall was the home of the Arderenes family until 1823 when it was purchased by a bank. Its stained-glass window shows several coats of arms, including the county borough of Stockport and the county of Chester.

BELOW: **FAIREY ENGINEERING, CROSSLEY ROAD, 1977.** The Crossley plant was set up in 1907 by Francis and William Crossley to extend their engine manufacturing business by building aircraft. The road adjacent to the factory was originally called Burnham Road. Later the name was changed to Crossley Street since the company felt that "Burnham" might be mistaken for "burn'em" — not too flattering when linked to their products. The plant was bought by Fairey Aviation in 1934.

LEFT: **VULCAN LORRY, c 1925.** A tram guard stands beside a Vulcan lorry in Mersey Square, Stockport. The Vulcan Motor and Engineering Company, based in Southport, first started building cars then commercial vehicles like the lorry shown here. Much of the cabin and flatbed at the rear was made of wood.

Right: **MAULDETH HALL, BURNAGE, 1925.** An aerial view of Mauldeth Hall, originally the home of the first bishop of Manchester. The hall was converted to a hospital for injured servicemen during the First World War. Later it became a hospital. It is now being restored as part of a housing development.

Below: **AIR RAID SHELTERS, STOCKPORT, 1939.** The Mayor of Stockport officially opens the bomb shelters beneath Chestergate. These shelters, 60ft below ground, often accommodated 7,000 people a night during the bombing raids of the Second World War. The shelters have now been restored and are open to the public.

Left: **STOCKPORT, 1909.** A rooftop view of Stockport from above Brinksway. The town was an important crossroads for north-south traffic; in the distance is the well-loved railway viaduct built in 1840 which dominates the western approaches to the town and carries the Manchester to London line.

Above: **STOCKPORT INFIRMARY, 1945.** The Infirmary opened in 1834 to replace the old "Dispensary and House of Recovery" on Daw Bank which was becoming too small for the needs of the rapidly growing town. Due to a lack of funding it was not fully operational until 1836. Extra wings were added: a south wing in 1870 and a north wing in 1898. The site has now become luxury flats but the neo-classical facade has been preserved.

Left: **CARNIVAL, URMSTON, c 1920.** The Urmston, Flixton and Davyhulme Carnival was an important and well-loved fixture in the local calendar until recent years. The parade of dancers, floats, bands and costume-clad children started from Chassen Road, then made its way down Church Street, Station Road and then past the Trafford General Hospital to the carnival field at Woodsend.

LEFT: **URMSTON**, *c* 1905. Standing in Crofts Bank Road looking towards Davyhulme we can see the tree-lined pavements that are still there to this day. At the time this photograph was taken the area was changing dramatically, thanks to the development of Trafford Park into the largest industrial estate in the world.

BELOW LEFT: **ALTRINCHAM, 1900s**. The Old Market Place. BOTTOM: **ALTRINCHAM, 1911**. George, the son of King Edward VII, succeeded his father as king on May 10 and was crowned King George V on June 22 1911. All over the country thousands of people celebrated with processions similar to this one in Market Street, Altrincham.

BELOW RIGHT: **DAVYHULME DRINKERS**, *c* 1870. A group of locals gather outside the Nag's Head at Davyhulme Circle to take a glass of locally-brewed ale and discuss the day's events. A war memorial now stands facing the renovated public house.

*Acknowledgment*

Thanks to Sara, my eldest daughter, for all her help and support with the book.

*Dedication*

I have always had support and love from my mum and dad. I could not have done all that I have to date without their help. You will be with me always now and forever.

First published in 2009 by Myriad Books Limited
35 Bishopsthorpe Road London SE26 4PA
Photographs © Manchester City Library Archives and Local Studies Collection except for those on pages 31 (bottom) and 32 (all) which are © Trafford Local Studies Library
Text © Robert Gibb
www.gibbsbookshop.co.uk

ISBN 1 84746 263 4
EAN 978 1 84746 263 3

Designed by Jerry Goldie Graphic Design
Printed in China
www.myriadbooks.com